# Word Patterns

---
## Book 2
---

Peter and Joan Moss

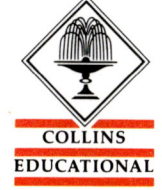

# Danger – dinosaurs

The naughty Noggle children, Nancy and Nick, got into the laboratory of Professor Nuttey, who lived next door. They climbed into the time machine they saw there, and switched the lever to 50 000 000 BC. Suddenly everything went black. There was a loud noise, and when they opened their eyes they saw......

Five minutes later it all went dark again, and then the lights in the room came on. Nancy and Nick raced from the room and told their mother what had happened.

Pretend you are Nick or Nancy. Tell the story of what you saw. Make it as real and as frightening as possible. Your teacher will help you to make a list of words you can use.

## Collective nouns

Sid collects stamps.

Brian collects badges.

Molly collects money.

A collection is a lot of the same kind of thing put together. There are some nouns which mean a collection of things. For example, a **crowd** of people, a **herd** of cows, a **team** of cricketers. We call words like crowd, herd, team **collective nouns**.

1. What kind of things go with these collective nouns?
   (a) a bunch of ——
   (b) a flock of ——
   (c) a gang of ——
   (d) a litter of ——
   (e) a swarm of ——

2. What collective noun would you use for these things?
   (a) —— of wolves
   (b) —— of soldiers
   (c) —— of elephants
   (d) —— of insects
   (e) —— of footballers

3. You now know three kinds of noun.
(a) **Proper nouns** – names of people and places and special things. They always start with a capital letter.
(b) **Common nouns** – names of ordinary things.
(c) **Collective nouns** – names of collections of things.

Sort these nouns out into the three kinds.

jennifer, gang, grass, banana, swarm, spain, forest, chocolate, glasgow, bunch, flock, christmas, crowd, table, thomas

| Proper nouns | Collective nouns | Common nouns |
|---|---|---|
| Jennifer | swarm | grass |

# Punctuation – just to remind you

Timmy did not listen in the lesson about punctuation. He thinks full stops, commas and question marks are monsters invented by teachers to trap boys and girls.

Sally listened carefully and worked hard. She knows that punctuation really helps to make her writing better.

This is what Timmy wrote.

sam rushed into the hall on his head he wore a cap pam came in slowly on her hands she wore red gloves.

This is what Sally wrote.

Sam rushed into the hall. On his head he wore a cap. Pam came in slowly. On her hands she wore red gloves.

**Timmy**

**Sally**

**Remember**

1. Every sentence starts with a capital letter.
2. Every sentence ends with a full stop unless it is a question.
   Most people like doing punctuation. Do you enjoy it?
3. In lists of things we put a comma between each complete thing except the last two. These are joined by 'and'.
   In our garden there are peas, beans, carrots, onions and weeds.

1. Put full stops, commas, question marks and capital letters in these sentences. Remember capital letters for proper nouns.
(a) did you see jane snooks yesterday
(b) she came to our house with bill bunge
(c) we all went to the sweet shop in banbury road
(d) we are going there again on friday
(e) can you come with us

2. Put full stops and capital letters in this paragraph. If you read it aloud your voice will drop where there should be a full stop. There are eight sentences.

the martian leader stared at mick and me he had never seen creatures with two eyes before all the martians had six eyes these were all round their heads the martians could see all ways at once they also had four arms the leader was a bright red colour he glowed in the dark

3. The Martian leader also had three mouths so that he could ask many questions at the same time. He did not wait for the answers. Write out what he said putting in all the question marks and capital letters. There are eight question marks.

is this planet earth what country is this is it japan how do you manage with only two eyes how do you know who is behind you why are you that funny colour is it difficult having only two hands can you get enough to eat with only one mouth.

5

# Alphabetical order     a b c d e f g h i j k l m n o p q r s t u v w x y z

Do you remember sorting words into alphabetical order in Book 1? By now you have learned so many words that most of the word piles are very big. Below you can see the 'a' pile. If you wanted to find a word it would take a long time, so we must sort them out again.

We know all of the words start with 'a' so now we look at the **second** letter in each of them. We put all the words that start with 'aa' in one heap, all those that start with 'ab' in another, all those with 'ac' in another, and so on. There may not be any words in some piles.

1. Use your dictionary to help you write down words beginning with 'a' followed by as many different second letters as possible.

aa ......     ab – able     ac – across

2. Put these words in alphabetical order of the **second** letter.
(a) secret  sleeve  sand  sting  scarf  soap  share  smile
(b) drag  dwarf  day  digger  dynamo  dust  deck  doctor
(c) twist  tap  turn  team  treat  think  toast  tight
(d) peep  plot  pin  public  phone  pond  pray  psalm

# Dictionary work

1. All of the underlined words have two or more meanings. Look up the words in your dictionary. Then write a sentence using the word with a different meaning from the one given on this page. Do it like this:

A stone will sink if you put it in water.
I put the dirty dishes in the sink.

(a) She cut off a lock of her hair.
(b) The final score was ten goals each.
(c) He was very patient as he waited in the rain.
(d) My leg is very tender where I bumped it.
(e) My father works in a coal mine.

2. There is something wrong in all of these sentences. Say what is wrong. For example:
The plumber came to mend the car which had broken down.
Plumbers mend pipes, not cars.

(a) The horizontal line sloped down to the left side.
(b) He was so generous he would never give anyone a penny.
(c) We bought a miniature car seven metres long.
(d) The comic was so funny we quaked with laughter.
(e) The robber lurked in the road where everyone could see him.

3. Find one word which you could use instead of those underlined. All of these are tricky to spell so use your dictionary.

(a) The ghost suddenly vanished from sight. (dis......)
(b) She was wearing rings, bracelets and necklaces. (jew......)
(c) Will you come on the day after Tuesday? (Wed......)
(d) The list with all the things to buy came by post. (cat......)
(e) That is so silly everyone will laugh at it. (ridic......)

7

# Joining words

All sorts of things can be joined together.

Bricks with mortar.   Cloth with stitches.   Paper with glue.   Teeth with toffee.

Do you remember in Book 1 you joined sentences together with 'and' and 'but'? You used 'and' to join two ordinary sentences, and 'but' when there was some difference between the sentences.

| We set out early. | We had a good time. | We set out early **and** we had a good time. |
| We set out early. | We soon came back. | We set out early **but** we soon came back. |

These joining words are called **conjunctions**.

1. Use 'and' or 'but' to join these pairs of sentences.
(a) Will you bring me a bag of chips? Put some vinegar on them.
(b) I love chips. I do not like fish.
(c) Get some for yourself too. Do not eat any of mine.
(d) Chips are my favourite food. I have them every day.
(e) I get them from the Friendly Friar. I like their pies too.

There are more conjunctions besides 'and' and 'but'. Look at these sentences.
(a) I met my friend. He was coming home from school.
(b) I held his coat. He climbed into the orchard.

We could use 'and' to join these pairs, but it would be much better if we said

(a) I met my friend **when** he was coming home from school.
(b) I held his coat **while** he climbed into the orchard.

'When' and 'while' are conjunctions here.

2. Here are some more conjunctions. Use them to join the pairs of sentences below.

since    because    while    until    although    before

(a) She kept on trying. She finally passed her test.
(b) We could not sleep. You were snoring so loudly.
(c) I could not beat him. He was much smaller than I was.
(d) You must tidy your bedroom. You go out at 9 o'clock.
(e) I do not feel very well. I ate the cake you made.
(f) I did all the washing up. You were watching television.

> You now know five different kinds of word:
> **common nouns** – names of ordinary things: bread, ball, button.
> **proper nouns** – names of people, places, special things: Bobby, York, Easter.
> **verbs** – doing words: begin, bite, breathe, bring.
> **adjectives** – describing words: black, beautiful, bare, blind.
> **conjunctions** – joining words: but, because, before, while.

There are three of each kind of word you know in the list below. Draw five columns in your book and sort the words out. Head the columns – common nouns, proper nouns, adjectives, verbs, conjunctions.

| because | butter | Blackpool | black | bite |
| white | when | word | write | Wilson |
| Anne | angry | argue | apple | and |

9

# Now we have got a nice exercise

'Got' and 'nice' are useful words but we all use them too much. There are many other words which are much better.

Here is Lazy Lucy writing in her diary.

> I **got** up at 7.30 and **got** dressed. When I **got** downstairs my mother had **got** breakfast for me. Then I **got** ready for school. I **got** on the bus and **got** off at the gates.

Lucy could have used different words for 'got' or left it out.

> I got up at 7.30 and **dressed**. When I **came** downstairs my mother **had** breakfast ready for me. Then I **prepared** for school. I **boarded** the bus and got off at the gates.

1. Write out this paragraph with as few 'got's as you can.

We have **got** a dog called Crawlie, but she has **got** fleas. Dad **got** some powder to kill them. We **got** her in the bath, and then we **got** some old towels to dry her. We **got** her into the garden and put the powder on her. She **got** angry, and then **got** loose. She **got** into the garden next door and it was ages before we **got** her back again.

2. 'Nice' is another lazy word. We could use instead words like pleasant, enjoyable, good, tasty, interesting, happy, delicious. Write out this paragraph putting in different words for 'nice'.

Saturday was such a **nice** day that I got up **nice** and early. After a **nice** breakfast I went for a **nice** walk. My friend came with me and we had a **nice** talk about school. We both said that English was a **nice** subject and Mrs Wurdie was a **nice** teacher.

10

# The strange spell

Ned and Deb love reading. Every Saturday morning they go to the old junk market because there is a stall which sells old books very cheaply. This is what happened last Saturday.
Write the story in four paragraphs. Use the pictures to help you with the first three, and make up your own ending for the last one.
When you have finished, draw a picture to show what happened.

search, ancient, tattered, fade, old, dirty rubbish, cheap, interesting, torn, useless

puzzled, dictionary, scribble, clues, old-fashioned, spelling, missing, strange

chemicals, sprinkle, stir, powder, seeds, bubble, poured, kitchen, smells, recipe

Was it a real spell? Did it make them taller, or shorter, or invisible? Did it turn them into something else? Did nothing happen at all? Perhaps there was an explosion. Try to make your ending as exciting and interesting as you can.

## Spot the differences

Our artist still cannot copy properly. When we asked him to copy the picture on the left hand side of the page he made ten mistakes. Can you see them? When you have found them, write them out like (a) below.

(a) The house on the left has five windows, the one on the right has only four.

Our artist cannot even do one picture properly. We asked him to draw a seaside scene, and this is what he drew. There are ten mistakes. Can you see them. Write them out like (a) below.

(a) The umbrella is upside down.

# Hey ho, hey hoo: a hard page work to do

1. Write down what people, animals or things you would put into these collections.

   (a) a herd of ……
   (b) a pack of ……
   (c) a squad of ……
   (d) a crowd of ……
   (e) a bundle of ……
   (f) a pride of ……

2. These are the names of some towns and villages in Britain. Put them in alphabetical order. Row (a) all start with 'B', so you will have to use the second letter. Row (b) all start with 'Fe' so you will have to use the third letter to put them into alphabetical order.

   (a) B<u>y</u>fleet, B<u>a</u>ngor, B<u>u</u>chan, B<u>i</u>bury, B<u>r</u>acknell, B<u>l</u>aby, B<u>o</u>cking, B<u>e</u>ccles.
   (b) Fe<u>n</u>gate, Fe<u>a</u>therstone, Fe<u>w</u>son, Fe<u>c</u>kenham, Fe<u>t</u>cham, Fe<u>e</u>ring, Fe<u>l</u>ixstowe, Fe<u>r</u>hilly.

3. Join these pairs of sentences with the conjunctions given below. They are not in the right order.

   and    because    before    when

   (a) It was 6 am. We set off on our holidays.
   (b) We travelled for ten hours. We reached the campsite.
   (c) I was very tired. It had been a very long journey.
   (d) I had my supper. I went straight to bed.

4. Write out these sentences without using 'nice' or 'got'.
   I **got** a **nice** surprise when the postman came. He is a very **nice** man and he had **got** a letter for me. I **got** excited and opened it quickly. But I **got** a shock. It was not a **nice** letter. It was from the library and they said I had **got** to pay 50p fine on a book which was overdue.

13

# Verbs

In Book 1 you learned that words which tell us what people or things are doing are called **verbs**.

Sleep   shout   hear   move   think   see

are all verbs. Often verbs have 'ed' on the end or change in another way to make in the past. For example

slept   shouted   heard   moved   thought   saw

are verbs as well.

### The verb test

To find out whether a word is a verb or not, try the 'Can I do it?' test. Ask yourself, 'Can I ......?' If you can, then the word is a verb. Which of these words are verbs?   run, very, eat, serious

Can you say 'I run'? Yes. Then 'run' is a verb.
Can you say 'I very'? No. Then 'very' is not a verb.
Can you say 'I eat'? Yes. Then 'eat' is a verb.
Can you say 'I serious'? No. Then 'serious' is not a verb.

1. Write out all the verbs in this paragraph. There are eight. We go on holiday to Yorkshire every year. Usually we stay in a guest house. I walk in the hills but I prefer the seaside. Sometimes we visit my cousins who live in Filey. Then we swim in the sea and sail in the bay.

2. Here are six 'breaking' verbs. We use each of them to show a special kind of breaking. Make up a sentence for each of them to show just what each verb really means.

crash     split     break     burst     crumble     squash

## Am, is, are, was, were – the 'being' verb

These words are part of the very important verb 'to be', though they do not seem to be 'doing' words. You can use them by themselves:
I <u>am</u> nine. You <u>were</u> greedy. She <u>was</u> sick. They <u>are</u> here. You can also use them to help make other verbs with 'ing' on the end. Both of the underlined words are part of the verb:
I <u>am going</u> today. We <u>were playing</u> tag. She <u>is trying</u> hard.

Make up sentences of your own
(a) using am, is, are, was and were as verbs on their own.
   I **am** clever. They **are** silly. She **was** brilliant.
(b) using them with other words to make verbs ending in 'ing'.
   She **was singing** like a parrot. I **am feeling** happy.

4. Write out the whole verb in these sentences. It will be two words: is, am, are, was, were and an 'ing' word.
(a) He is going to school tomorrow.
(b) I am hoping to win that race.
(c) We are doing all of the work ourselves.
(d) The class were struggling to learn about verbs.

I **am** clever.

He **is** silly.

# Verbs with add-ons

Bertie has a bicycle. It is just an ordinary bicycle, and not very exciting. He goes to Charlie's Cycle Shop where there are all sorts of add-on gadgets. He gets what he wants and fixes it to his bicycle. Now his bike certainly is more exciting.

You can do with verbs what Bertie did with his bicycle. Here are sentences with ordinary verbs. They are not very interesting.

> I **walked** along the road.     She **ate** her soup.

Now let us put in some 'add-on' words.

I walked **slowly** along the road.     She ate her soup **greedily**.
I walked **quickly** along the road.    She ate her soup **noisily**.

These add-on words for verbs are called **adverbs**. They tell us how the verb was done – walked **quickly**......ate **greedily**.

Many 'how' adverbs end in 'ly'. Sometimes they are put after their verb, and sometimes they are separated by other words.

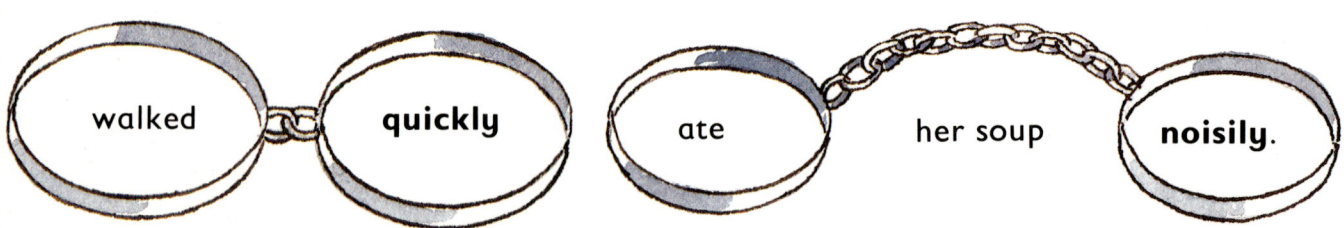

16

Read this dull little story.

She swam to the island. She climbed to the top of a little hill and sat in the shade of a tree. The seagulls cried all round her. She tried to see her friends on the shore, and when she did she waved to them.

Now we will put some 'how' adverbs in to improve it.

She swam **quickly** to the island. She climbed **slowly** to the top of a little hill and sat **comfortably** in the shade of a tree. The seagulls cried all around her **noisily**. She tried **hard** to see her friends on the shore, and when she did, she waved to them **frantically**.

1. Write a sentence saying what each of the people on this page are doing. You must have a verb and an adverb.
(a) He stared **angrily** at the wasp that had stung him.

2. Here are five adverbs. Put them in the sentences below.

rudely   suddenly   slowly   quickly   loudly

(a) Fanny went ...... along the path because she was late.
(b) She climbed ...... up the tree because she was scared of heights.
(c) The branch collapsed ...... and she fell to the ground.
(d) Fanny shouted ...... to her friend Pat for help.
(e) Pat answered ...... that it served her right for being late.

3. Use these adverbs in sentences of your own. Make sure they answer the question, 'How did he or she do the verb?'

carefully   safely   sadly   angrily   alone

17

# Can you tell me the way please?

This is a map of your town. You are standing at the place marked A. Several strangers ask if you can tell them the way to different places in the town. Write down what you would tell them. For example:

"Can you tell me the way to the Burger Bar, please?"
"Go straight along the High Street, past Alfred Street. Go over the traffic lights and turn left at the next road, which is Worble Street. The Burger Bar is on your right."

(a) The swimming pool        (b) The town hall
(c) The railway station      (d) The museum
(e) The supermarket          (f) The church

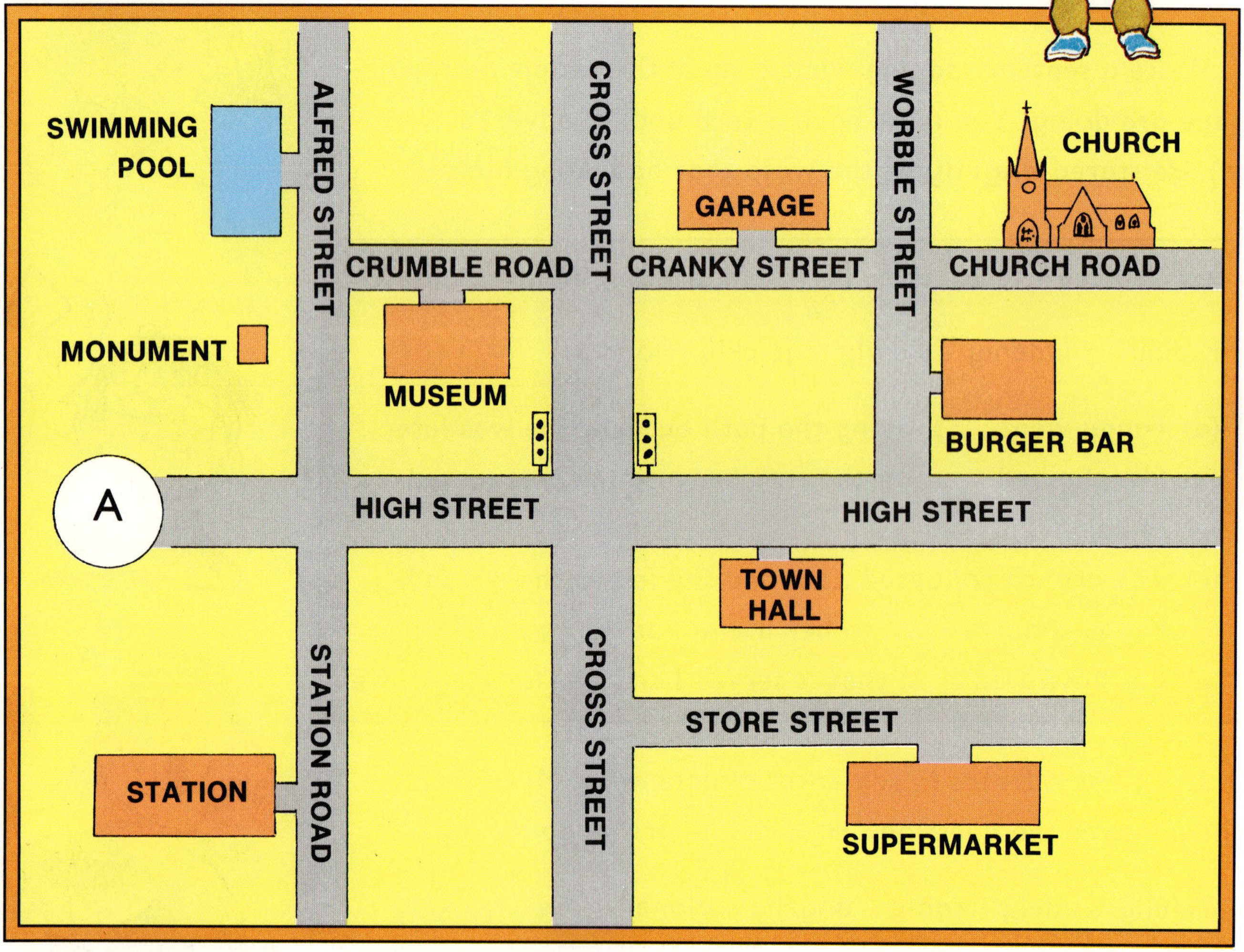

18

# Yet another hard work page

1. Put 'was' or 'were' in these sentences.
   (a) When we —— smaller we thought you and Jim —— giants.
   (b) Jim really —— tall, but you —— no bigger than I ——.
   (c) It was fun because where we —— living there —— plenty of things to do.
   (d) There —— the park and there —— the woods where there —— lots of trees to climb.

2. Adverbs usually tell us how a verb was done. Many adverbs end in 'ly'. Pick out the adverbs in these sentences and say which verbs they tell us more about. For example
   (a) The temperature dropped sharply on January 3rd.

   | **Adverb** | **Verb** |
   |---|---|
   | (a) sharply | dropped |

   (b) The snow fell heavily during the night.
   (c) The ground was thickly covered by morning.
   (d) The children dressed quickly and rushed eagerly outside.
   (e) Jane tripped clumsily and fell headlong into a big snowdrift.

3. Here are some sentences and phrases. Pick out the phrases and make them into sentences by adding some more words.
   (a) We break up next Wednesday.
   (b) in the morning
   (c) because of the fog
   (d) It is time to go now.
   (e) before the rain
   (f) in your exercise books

Word Mine

# Time machine to the future

You have all seen TV programmes about time machines. People sometimes go into the past and meet dinosaurs. Sometimes they go into the future and meet robots and Martians. Verbs can go into the past and the future too.

Do you remember about sending verbs into the past?
Sometimes we add 'ed' on the end:
Today I **live** in Newcastle. Last year I **lived** in Hull.
Sometimes we change some of the letters of the verb:
Today I **buy** a tiger. Yesterday I **bought** an elephant.

When we want to take a verb into the future, it is not strong enough to go on its own. It needs a helper word. The helper word we use to make verbs into the future is **will**.

Seven years ago I **rode** in my pushchair.

Today I **ride** on my new bicycle.

In ten years I **will ride** in my sports car.

20

1. Write these sentences in the future. Start with 'Tomorrow......' instead of 'Today......'
(a) Today Ann goes into the garden.
(b) She picks some flowers for the house.
(c) She grabs a nettle by mistake.
(d) It stings her hand badly.
(e) She thinks that plastic flowers are best.

The words 'am', 'is' and 'are' are parts of the verb 'to be'. They are different from most other verbs, which make the future by adding 'will' to the verb itself. The parts 'is', 'am' and 'are' all change into 'will be'.

Today I **am** a bad boy, but tomorrow I **will be** worse.
Now we **are** hungry. In six hours we **will be** starving.

2. Finish these sentences in any way you like.
All the verbs must be in the future.
I think that in the future
(a) schools **will have** robots for teachers.
(b) school clothes......
(c) school meals......
(d) the lessons......

3. Fill in the blank spaces in this chart.

| Past | Present | Future |
|---|---|---|
| —— | I am | —— |
| we jumped | —— | —— |
| —— | —— | we will sing |
| —— | they are | —— |
| she flew | —— | —— |
| he got | —— | —— |

21

# Writing Letters

Imagine you live in a flat in a large city. Your Uncle Ben and Aunt Meg have invited you to stay on their farm for part of your summer holidays.

You could easily telephone your aunt and uncle, but they would much prefer a letter. You could write something like this.

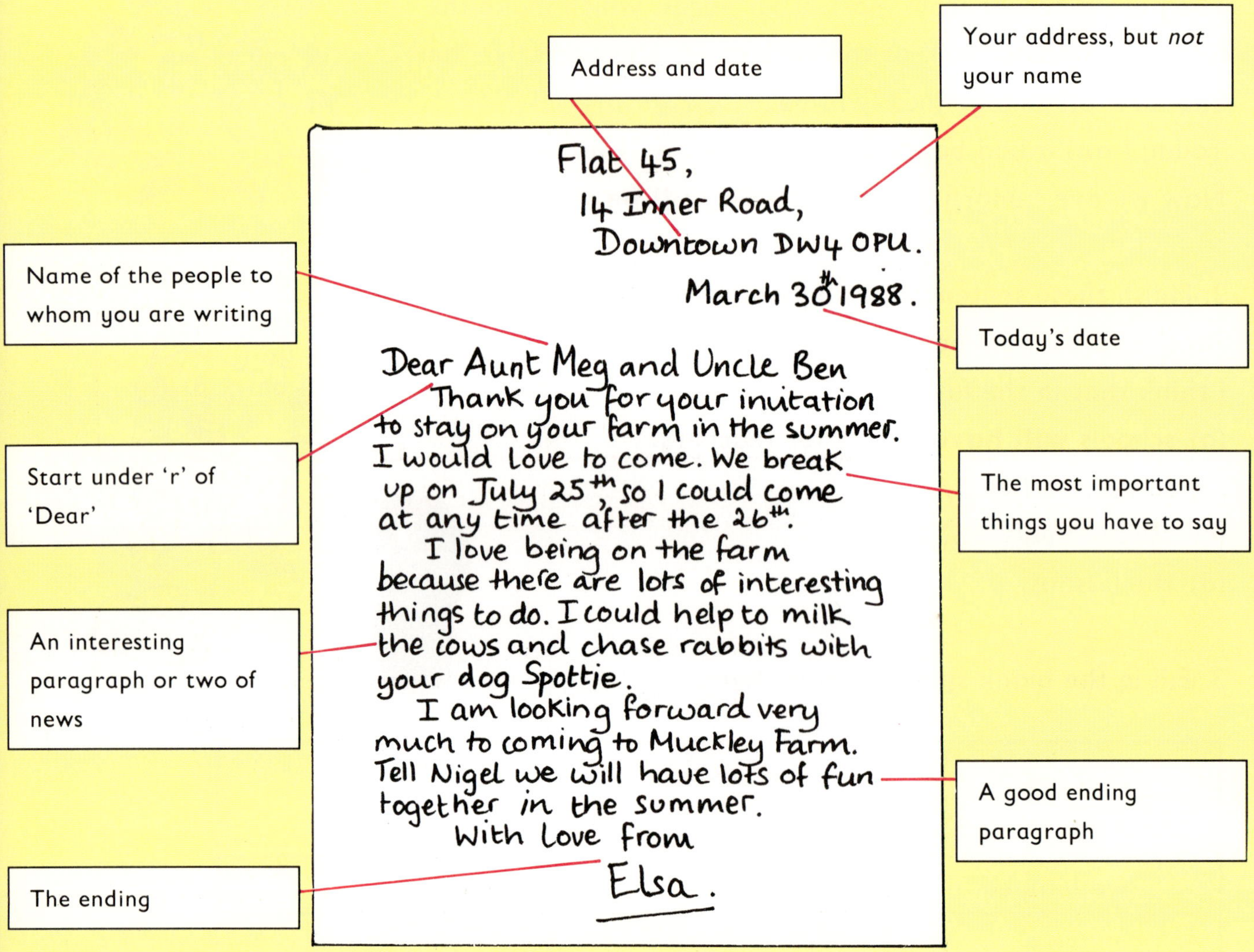

---

**Address and date**

**Your address, but *not* your name**

**Today's date**

**Name of the people to whom you are writing**

**Start under 'r' of 'Dear'**

**The most important things you have to say**

**An interesting paragraph or two of news**

**A good ending paragraph**

**The ending**

> Flat 45,
> 14 Inner Road,
> Downtown DW4 0PU.
> March 30th 1988.
>
> Dear Aunt Meg and Uncle Ben
>   Thank you for your invitation to stay on your farm in the summer. I would love to come. We break up on July 25th so I could come at any time after the 26th.
>   I love being on the farm because there are lots of interesting things to do. I could help to milk the cows and chase rabbits with your dog Spottie.
>   I am looking forward very much to coming to Muckley Farm. Tell Nigel we will have lots of fun together in the summer.
>     With love from
>       Elsa.

1. Write to your cousin Nigel inviting him to stay with you in your flat in the centre of the city. You should have three paragraphs like this:

(a) The invitation asking him to come. Suggest some suitable dates. You should say that your parents' flat is not as big as Muckley Farm, and he may have to sleep somewhere unusual.

(b) Tell him some of the things he might like to do in the city. He does not often get a chance to visit shops, cinemas, museums, ice-rinks and so on.

(c) Write a good ending, saying how much you are looking forward to seeing him.

## Envelopes

Your aunt and uncle probably would not mind too much if you made some mistakes in your letter, but the envelope is very important. You must get it right or the postman may not know where to deliver it.

2. Draw two envelopes in your exercise book, 16 cms × 11 cms. Address the first one to your home address, and the second to a friend who lives somewhere else.

# 'Place' words

Oxy-hydro-alpha-beta-choro-hexabutylene

That sounds a very important word, but it is really just the scientists' name for a kind of plastic. For most people these little words are much more important:

to   in   at   on   from   into   through
over   under   above   around   towards

Imagine someone telephoned you and said, "Be sure you ride your bicycle ---- school today," and then rang off. You did not hear the word between 'bicycle' and 'school'. Any of the words in the list above would fit in. The one you chose would make a lot of difference to the meaning of the message.

These important little 'place' words are called **prepositions**.

to school

through school

in school

under school

over school

Put these prepositions in the sentences below. You will have to use some of them more than once.

from   over   above   through   to   in   on   into   across

(a) Peggy went ...... the Post Office to get an airmail stamp.
(b) She stuck it ...... the letter for her brother ...... Canada.
(c) She put the letter ...... the posting box and then went ...... the door ...... the street.
(d) The letter was taken ...... the post office ...... the airport.
(e) It was put ...... a plane which flew high ...... the clouds.
(f) It flew ...... the Atlantic and arrived ...... Canada the next day.

24

## Oh dear! Another hard work page

1. Write out these sentences putting two words in place of all those underlined. The first letters are given to help you.

   (a) All the <u>dictionaries, encyclopaedias and atlases</u> are on the top shelf. (ref...... b......)

   (b) The school taught <u>French, German and Spanish</u>. (for..... lan......)

   (c) The houses on this side are all <u>numbers like 1, 3, 5, 7, 9, 11</u>. (o...... num......)

   (d) The Open Road Shop sells <u>tents, sleeping bags, folding tables and chairs, gas stoves</u>. (cam...... eq......)

2. Write this paragraph in the future. You will have to change all of the underlined verbs. Start with 'Tomorrow we......'

Yesterday we <u>had</u> a big party. All the class <u>were</u> invited. We <u>ate</u> a huge tea and then we <u>went</u> to the fair. We <u>spent</u> about a pound each on rides. At nine o'clock our parents <u>brought</u> us home and we <u>went</u> to bed.

3. Adjectives are describing words which tell us more about nouns. There are eight adjectives in this paragraph. Write them down and say which nouns they describe.

The old beggar wore tattered clothes. His black coat was tied up with string. His dirty shirt had huge holes in it. His thin trousers did not keep out the bitter weather. His heavy boots had no laces in them.

| **Adjective** | **Noun** |
|---|---|
| old | beggar |

# A page of cats

1. Put adjectives in the blank spaces to make these cats sound interesting.

(a) A …… cat with a ……, …… hat.

(b) A ……, …… cat on a ……, …… mat.

(c) A ……, …… cat dancing with a ……, …… rat.

2. All of these words start with 'cat'. What are they?
   (a) This cat is a very big church. cathedral
   (b) This cat has lots of legs.
   (c) This cat is a lot of cows.
   (d) You do this cat when you play ball.

3. Here is a long 'cat' word. It means a terrible disaster. See how many other words you can make from it.

| catastrophe ||| 
|---|---|---|
| 3-letter words | 4-letter words | 5-letter words |

4. What do these mean?

(a) It is raining cats and dogs.

(b) She is a copy cat.

# Fat cat

Siamese have cobalt eyes, their tails are thin and kinky,
Siamese are slender, Siamese are slinky,
The experts are agreed on that –
They haven't seen this family cat.

His fur is sleek, his eyes are blue,
His pedigree is long and true –
But what a figure! What a weight!
And how he eats! At what a rate!
For pussy hasn't read the books,
He doesn't know how wrong he looks.

Left-over yoghurt, frozen peas,
Spaghetti, any kind of cheese,
He wolfs them down (if that's the word)
Then ups and outs and grabs a bird.
He sits below the baby's chair
To catch the dropped bits in the air,
The phone rings and you turn your back,
He's on the table, snicker snack.

We tried to keep him slim and lean,
He got bad-tempered, scratchy, mean,
And used to tour the neighbour's bins
And leave the bits – fish bones and skins –
On our front doorstep. And one time
He stole their Sunday joint, a crime
We felt must be prevented;
So now he's fat, full and contented,
The Siamese who over-ate,
Our greedy, gross, unusual pet.

Mary Rayner

# Saying words

He said, "Help! I am afraid of mice."

He said. "Hush. It is a big secret."

She said, "Stop!......, Stop, Thief!"

He said, "Please may I have some more?"

All day long we talk. Sometimes we speak in a loud voice, sometimes in a quiet one. Sometimes we use words when we are angry, or when we are frightened. We may want to tell someone something, or we may want to ask them a question.

When you speak people usually know by your voice what you are feeling. When you write what people say, you must explain how they felt when they spoke. Try not to use 'said' every time because it does not tell us how the people spoke.

If you were writing about the people in the drawings at the top of the page it would be much better to put
He **screamed**, 'Help! I am afraid of mice'.
She **whispered**, 'Hush. It is a big secret'.
She **yelled**, 'Stop!......Stop, Thief!'
He **asked**, 'Please may I have some more?'

1. Here are some saying words. Put them into the sentences below.   asked   called   grumbled   whispered   sobbed

(a) The policeman ——, "What is the matter?"

(b) The little boy ——, "I'm lost."

(c) Tom ——, "It is not fair. I have to clean up every day."

(d) He —— in Bill's ear, "I'll put a drawing pin on his chair."

(e) The teacher ——, "Stop talking and get on with your work."

28

# The ghosts of Grisley Grange.

Thomas and Geraldine (Tom and Gerry) were being shown round the ruined Grisley Grange. When the guide went round the corner, Gerry turned a strange knob on the wall. Suddenly the floor opened, and the two children shot downwards. When they came to a stop they were in a brightly-lit room with a lot of skeletons jabbering...... Write the story of what happened. There will be four paragraphs — one for each picture.

skeletons   capture   dragged
satchel   bony   rattling   squeaky

crocodile   magician   cauldron
steaming   bubbling   snakes   toad

# Saying without words

We often say, or write, far too many words. Sometimes we do not need any words at all and can use signs.

If you saw these three signs you would know what to do at once.

  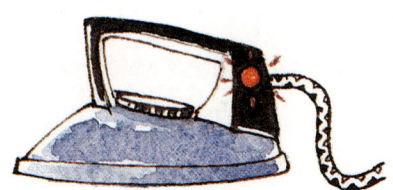

Stop the car or bicycle. There is danger ahead.

Road repairs ahead. Go where the blue arrow points.

The electricity is on. Take care you do not burn yourself.

Now look at these signs. What do they mean and what would you do if you saw them? Write sentences to explain what each sign means.

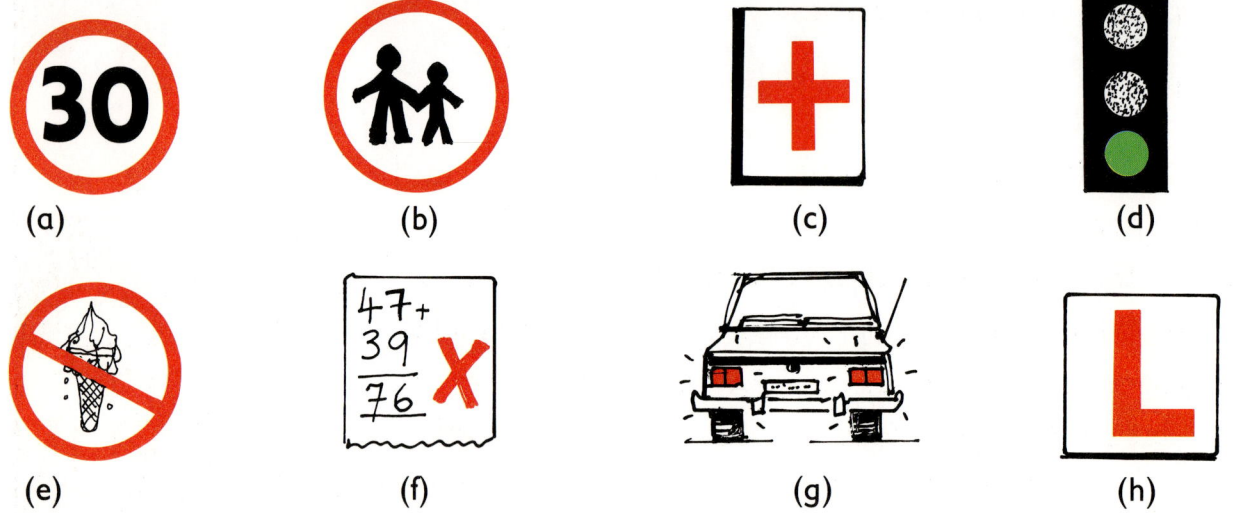

## You know what this page is!

1. Write out five questions of your own. They could be riddles. Start with one of these words. Do not forget capital letters and question marks.

why    when    who    where    what

2. This paragraph is written in the future. Write it out again changing all of the underlined verbs to the past. Start 'Yesterday Mary ......'

Tomorrow Mary will visit Betty in hospital. Jill will go with her. They will take some fruit and some 'Get well' cards which our class will make. Betty will be glad to see them.

3. Change the underlined words in these sentences to the opposite. Do not use any word twice.
(a) It was cold and the sea was rough.
(b) Ben was unhappy because Daniel had gone away.
(c) He made a small sandcastle and put a few shells on it.
(d) His sandwiches were thick and the tea was cold.
(e) He felt miserable and went home early.

4. Here are five 'moving' verbs.

hop    kicked    pulled    hobbled    stepped

Write out this paragraph putting the best word in each space.
Bill ...... the ball so hard that he hurt his ankle. He ...... over to Miss Brown. She took off his shoe and told him to ...... back to school. Daren ...... open the door for him, but ...... back on Bill's good foot.

# Pronouns

In fairy stories witches and wizards can change themselves into all sorts of things whenever they want to. But whatever they become, they are still the same person.

Nouns can do this too. Look at these sentences.

Jack asked Jill, "Will Jill ask Jane to give that toffee to Jack?"
Jill said to Jack, "Jill will not ask Jane to give the toffee to Jack."
You would not write that, would you? You would write:
Jack asked Jill, "Will <u>you</u> ask Jane to give that toffee to <u>me</u>?"
<u>She</u> said to <u>him</u>, "<u>I</u> will not ask <u>her</u> to give <u>it</u> to <u>you</u>."
The names Jack, Jill, Jane and toffee all change to something else, like the wizards, but they are still Jack, Jill, Jane and toffee.

Jack calls Jill 'you' and himself 'me'.
Jill calls Jack 'you' and herself 'I'.
Jill calls Jane 'her' and the toffee 'it'.

All of these words, 'I', 'me', 'you', 'her' and 'it' take the place of the nouns Jack, Jill, Jane and toffee. We call them **pronouns**. These are some of the most important ones.

1. Put pronouns in place of the underlined words in these sentences.
   (a) Maggie has a typewriter. Mr Tappit gave the typewriter to Maggie.
   (b) Mr Tappit asked Maggie to write some letters for Mr Tappit.
   (c) Maggie typed the letters for Mr Tappit.
   (d) Mr Tappit said, "Maggie has done very well. Mr Tappit and Maggie will go and have coffee if there is any left."

2. Write a story with four paragraphs about these pictures. You can be one of the children or one of the monsters. Underline the pronouns when you have finished. You could start:
We were on the beach one day when I saw a bottle. It was……

# Belonging apostrophes

A comma above the line is called an **apostrophe**.
It can show belonging.

> **Rule 1.** When we want to show that something belongs to <u>one</u> person or thing, we add <u>'s</u> after the name of the person or thing.
> The ears belonging to the horse – the horse's ears.
> The shoes belonging to Tom – Tom's shoes.

1. Rewrite these sentences so that they have a belonging apostrophe.
   (a) The game belonging to Peter.
   (b) The hat belonging to Hattie.
   (c) The wand belonging to the wizard.
   (d) The cauldron belonging to the witch.
   (e) The idea that Ivan had.
   (f) The voice of the teacher.

pig's tail

2. Put belonging apostrophes in these sentences. Make sure you put it only on the belonging word, and not on other words which end in 's'. For example,

Sally's socks have red stripes.

(a) Johns sister Jill is a strange girl.
(b) She knitted a cover for her dogs tail.
(c) Jills favourite food is boiled cabbage and ice cream.
(d) She made a scarf for her friends budgie.
(e) She never obeys her mothers wishes.

Tom's teeth

Tessa's T-shirt

**Rule 2.** When something belongs to more than one person or thing we put an apostrophe **after** the last 's'. The word will already have an 's' at the end because it is a plural noun.
The collars belonging to four dogs – Four dogs' collars.
The chatter of five monkeys – Five monkeys' chatter.

The cat's whiskers. (Whiskers belonging to one cat. Apostrophe before the 's' because there is only one cat.)

The cats' curls. (Curls belonging to two cats. Apostrophe after the letter 's' because 'cats' is plural.)

The fighting cats. (No apostrophe at all because there is nothing belonging to the cats.)

3. Rewrite these phrases putting in apostrophes like the ones above.
   (a) The work of many pupils.     (d) The spells of three witches.
   (b) The eyes of six parrots.     (e) The footmarks of four foxes.
   (c) The efforts of all the girls. (f) The orders of two bosses.

4. Put belonging apostrophes in these sentences. They will all come after the 's'.
   (a) The two knights horses trotted along the path.
   (b) The horses hooves clattered on the stones.
   (c) Suddenly the knights heard the sound of many dragons wings.
   (d) They heard the noise of the monsters teeth snapping together.
   (e) They saw great flames coming from the beasts nostrils.
   (f) The three wise magicians spell had come true.

# How do you make it work?

When you get a new toy or gadget there are instructions on how to use it. Sometimes they are in pictures, sometimes in words and sometimes in both, as for the electric car below.

1. Make sure the starting lever on the side of the car is pointing to 'S'.

2. Lift the lid of the battery box using the little knob on the top of the car.

3. Put in a battery with the end (marked +) at the front.

4. Close the lid of the battery box. Make sure it is tightly closed.

5. Move the starting lever to 'G' to start the car moving.

6. Move the lever to 'S' to stop the car.

You are sending some orangeade to a friend on Mars who has never seen it before. These are the drawings which show how to open the tin. Write out the instructions in words like the ones above.

1.  2.  3.  4.

36

## More hard work

1. Use some of these pronouns to replace the underlined words in these sentences.

I   me   we   us   you   it   he
him   she   her   they   them

James is talking.

(a) James told Becca that Becca was silly.
(b) Becca hit James and Becca and James had a fight.
(c) Mummy told Becca and James to stop fighting.
(d) Mummy said, "Mummy, James and Becca will go to the shops."
(e) A walk will do Mummy, James and Becca good."

2. ur, er and ir make the same sound. curl, girl, fern

Write out these words putting in the right letters. Check the spelling in your dictionary.

(a) You are a boy, not a g––l.
(b) Something hot will b––n.
(c) A man wears a sh––t.
(d) A quick pull is a j––k.
(e) First, second and th––d.
(f) You put your money in a p––se.
(g) Drink when you are th––sty.
(h) A n––se looks after sick people.

3. Write out these sentences to show that one person is the owner. For example, a boy's cap.

(a) Johns books are untidy.
(b) Rachels clothes are smart.
(c) Wendys toys are broken.
(d) Errols shoes need cleaning.
(e) Alices knees are knobbly.
(f) A cats eyes are green.

# Comparing Adjectives

When we look at **two** things and say that one is bigger, or smaller, or better or thinner than the other we say we are **comparing** them.

Tom is **fat** but Peter is **fatter**.

Dick is **skinny** but Rick is **skinnier**.

John is **poor** but Sam is **poorer**.

'Fat', 'skinny' and 'poor' are all adjectives.
We call 'fatter', 'skinnier' and 'poorer' the **comparative** of the adjectives, 'fat', 'skinny' and 'poor'.

When we compare two things, we add 'er' or 'r' to the adjective.
For adjectives ending in 'y' change the 'y' into 'i' and add 'er'.
What has happened to fat?

1. Write out these sentences putting in the comparative of the underlined adjective.
   (a) The chair is hard but the floor is ......
   (b) The armchair is soft but the settee is ......
   (c) The wallpaper is pretty but the pictures are ......
   (d) The radiator is hot but the stove is ......
   (e) Question 2 is tricky but 3 is even ......

2. Make up six sentences of your own like the ones above. Use the adjectives below and their comparatives.

angry   fast   lazy   quiet   ugly   heavy   tame

# Yours and mine

The words 'mine', 'ours', 'hers', 'his', 'yours' and 'theirs' are in place of the nouns illustrated above.
Words which stand in place of nouns are called pronouns. But these are a special kind of pronoun because they show belonging. They are called **possessive pronouns** because 'possess' means that something belongs to someone.
**Note**: possessive pronouns **never** have an apostrophe, although they show belonging.

        **Never** write   our's   your's   her's

1. Write out these sentences putting the possessive pronouns in place of the underlined words. In (a) and (b) you will have to add the words in brackets.

      his   hers   mine   ours   yours

(a) This book (is) belongs to me. That one (is) belongs to you.
(b) Here (are) the books that belong to both of us.
(c) We will share these apples. These big ones are the ones that belong to us.
(d) The maggoty ones are the ones that belong to you.
(e) Sally has taken the ones we gave to her.
(f) Sam has taken the ones that we gave to him.

---

our's ✗

your's ✗

her's ✗

ours ✓

yours ✓

hers ✓

# Peculiar plurals

You remember that to make plurals you usually add 's' to the word.

One school ... three schools.   A house ... many houses.

Words which end in ssssh-ing sounds add 'es'.

One box ... two boxes.   A fish ... many fishes.
A witch ... two witches.

There are a few words, however, which do not obey these rules.

| Nouns that end in 'f' or 'fe' change to 'ves'. | Nouns ending in a consonant and 'y' change to 'ies'. | Some nouns obey no rules. You just have to learn them. |
|---|---|---|
| wolf   wolves | baby   babies | woman   women |
| thief   thieves | cry   cries | man   men |
| leaf   leaves | gipsy   gipsies | child   children |
| knife   knives | fly   flies | mouse   mice |
| half   halves | puppy   puppies | goose   geese |
| loaf   loaves | lady   ladies | ox   oxen |
| wife   wives | sky   skies | |

Do not forget that words which end in a vowel + 'y' just add s.

Write out these sentences changing all the underlined words into the plural.

(a) The man and woman bought flowers from the gipsy.
(b) The child played with the toy on the tray.
(c) The huge fly bit the pony, the donkey and the wolf.
(d) The thief stole the gold leaf from the magic tree.

# Don't get into a rage, its a hard work page

1. Put 'a' or 'an' in front of these nouns. Say them aloud first.

| flag | witch | army | pet | acrobat | orange |
| cake | egg | exercise | Indian | belt | hospital |

2. Write down the plurals of these words.

a car     two......　　a day     six......

one wife     three......　　one cherry     seven......

one jelly     four......　　one loaf     eight......

3. Compare Tony and Tom by filling in the spaces.

(a) Tom is <u>tall</u> but Tony is <u>taller</u>.　　(d) Tony is brave but Tom is ......

(b) Tony is strong, but Tom is ......　　(e) Tom is fat, but Tony is ......

(c) Tom is ugly but Tony is ......　　(f) Tony is quick but Tom is ......

4. Put these possessive pronouns in the spaces below.

         ours    yours    mine    hers    his

Bert and Becca are arguing about who owns the pet mouse.

(a) Bert said that it was ......

(b) Becca said that it was ...... really.

(c) Bert shouted, 'No. It is ...... It is not ......'

(d) Becca said, 'Let us share it then it will be ......'

5. Put adjectives in the blank spaces to make this paragraph more interesting. Think about the noise, the happy people and the bright colours at carnivals.

The ...... procession went along the ...... street. The ...... bands played very loudly. The people wore ...... costumes and waved ...... flags. There were ...... balloons floating everywhere. The ...... people danced and sang as they watched the ...... scene.

# Get rid of the waste

Many of us use far too many words.
This is how someone described 'Basher' Thugge.
He is a great, big, huge man with mighty, strong, powerful muscles.
'Great', 'big' and 'huge' all mean the same. So do 'mighty', 'strong' and 'powerful'.
So, we can leave out two from each list and say

He is a huge man with mighty muscles.

You could use either of the other words. You have to choose which one you think is best.

1. Write out these sentences leaving out words which are not needed.
(a) I saw a great, big, huge rat.
(b) There was a tiny, little, small flea on its back.
(c) The rat's den was a dark, black, inky hole in the ground.
(d) The rat ran very quickly at great speed to its den.
(e) When they got there the flea jumped down and got off the rat's back.
(f) The flea said, 'Thanks. That has saved me walking all the way on my feet.'
(g) The rat was annoyed, angry and furious.

> Do you know this old poem about fleas? 'Ad infinitum' are two Latin words which mean 'on and on for ever.'
> 
> Big fleas have smaller fleas,
> Upon their back to bite 'em.
> And smaller fleas have tinier fleas,
> And so ad infinitum.

# Make it short

Here are two people arguing about the television.

"Switch on the TV to BBC – there is a programme about the RAF."
"No. I want ITV to see the film about wildlife in the USA."

What the people really meant was

"Turn the television to the British Broadcasting Corporation as I want to watch the programme about the Royal Air Force."
"No. I want the Independent Television to see the film about wildlife in the United States of America."

When we shorten words like this we call them **abbreviations**.

Here are some common abbreviations.
BC = Before Christ.
PO = Post office.
AD = After Christ (Latin words Anno Domini).
UK = United Kingdom.
OHMS = On Her Majesty's Service (Government letters).

1. Write out in full what these sentences mean.
(a) The PO brought me a letter marked OHMS.
(b) Julius Caesar was killed in the year 43 BC.
(c) The city of Pompeii was destroyed in AD 79.
(d) The RAF plane flew non-stop from the USA to the UK.
(e) Our old TV will not get ITV – only BBC.

2. Can you find out what these abbreviations mean?

Dr.   AA   GB   DJ   mph   cm   MP   NHS   pm

# The sea egg

Jo and Toby are on holiday with their parents in Cornwall. Their holiday home is right on the beach and one day they buy a large egg-shaped object from a fisherman. They can hear tapping noises inside it, and leave it in a rock pool to hatch out. When they go to look for it, it has vanished, and a few days later they catch a glimpse of a young triton – a merman. They try to make friends with him, but he is afraid of them. Jo is speaking:

"I'm going to dress in seaweed. It will look more like a sea-person." Jo had a piece of string and was knotting sprays of loose seaweed on to it. He tied it on like an apron. Toby did the same with variations. He had a tail.

The little triton was hanging on to the edge of the pool to see better. Finally two acceptable sea-boys drew near, holding out their offerings, a spiral shell and a necklace.

As they lowered themselves into the water the triton submerged, but came up somewhere else, and presently, advancing slowly and retreating hurriedly like a puppy being coaxed by strangers, he grew bolder. Jo's necklace was snatched first. At a little distance it was fingered, clicked to make its bead music, sucked, and finally put on.

Toby's arm was aching with holding out the spiral shell when at last it was taken, and with a frisk of his two tails the triton disappeared. He surfaced again in a moment and sat on a rock to look at his treasure. He emptied the water out of it, balanced it by its point, twirling it on the end of his first finger, put it to his ear and listened to it with deep attention. He gave Toby a quick bewildering grin. Then holding the shell in both hands he put the wide end to his lips as if he were playing a flute, and blew. An eerie sound of great sweetness came out, not unlike a curlew's call but with a peculiar hollow shell quality that was unmistakeable.

L. M. Boston

1. Answer these questions in proper sentences.
(a) Why did Toby and Jo 'dress in seaweed'?
(b) What presents did they offer the triton to show they were friendly?
(c) Why was Toby's arm aching?
(d) How do you know the triton liked the presents?
(e) What is a flute?

2. What do these phrases mean?
(a) 'Advancing slowly and retreating hurriedly'
(b) 'with a frisk of his two tails'
(c) 'holding out offerings'
(d) 'an eerie sound'

3. Imagine that the triton led Jo and Toby to his home in a large underwater cave, first giving them magic powers to swim underwater for a long time. What do you think they saw? Were there just natural things like fish and seaweed, or were there magic things as well? Write a description of the cave, and then say what happened.

# Sounds the same

Look at these two hissing noises. They sound the same, but you can see they are very different in meaning.

There are many words in English which sound the same but have different meanings.

1. Put the right word from the pair in brackets in these sentences.
   (a) (Wear/where) do you (by/buy) the nice clothes you (wear/where).
   (b) I go over (there/their). You can (sea/see) the shop from (hear/here).
   (c) Oh – is it right (buy/by) the parking space (for/four) bikes?
   (d) Yes. If you go (two/to) the corner it is only (for/four) shops further down from (their/there).
   (e) I (here/hear) they have a sale, and (their/there) clothes are very cheap.
   (f) Yes. Perfect (for/four) your holiday (by/buy) the (see/sea).

2. Muzzi the Martian is on holiday on Earth. He is writing a postcard to his friend back on Mars. This is part of what he wrote. Can you write it out properly for him?
When you have finished, draw the picture you think was on the other side of Muzzi's card.

> You ask wear I have bean. I have bean for a week over their to sea the sea. There were boats on the see and I could here the waves. I am going to by some T-shirts for you to where with 'Earth' on them.
> Love Muzzi.

# The last hard work page this year

1. Write out these sentences putting in the right sound-alike word.
(a) If you stand (hear/here) you will (hear/here) the music.
(b) Climb up that (bare/bear) rock and you will see the (bare/bear).
(c) I would like to (be/bee) a (be/bee) making honey all day.
(d) Over (their/there) you can see (their/there) tree house.
(e) (Wear/where) did you buy those shoes you (wear/where) for jogging?
(f) It does not take more than (to/two) minutes (to/two) do it.

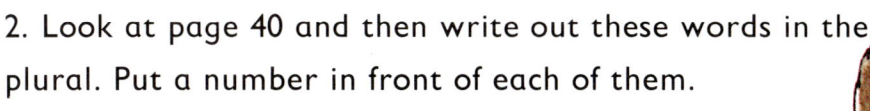

2. Look at page 40 and then write out these words in the plural. Put a number in front of each of them.
(a) box   (b) witch   (c) splash   (d) hiss   (e) switch
(f) monkey   (g) pony   (h) donkey   (i) fly   (j) sky

3. Put the possessive pronouns his, hers, mine, yours, theirs and ours in this silly poem.

*Greedy Kate cuts the birthday cake*
Welcome my friends to Snooty Towers,
This birthday cake it shall be ...... .
This fruity cake looks nice and fine,
The biggest piece it shall be ...... .
Belinda Jane, my little niece,
...... shall be a tiny piece.

Baby Frank, who sucks his thumb,
...... shall be a little crumb.
Come my friends, and use your claws,
Whatever's left, it shall be ...... .
My mum and dad, who are upstairs,
An empty plate it shall be ...... .

4. This is the last exercise in Book 2. Do a funny drawing for the cover of Book 3 which you may have next term. It should have something to do with writing English.

# Index

| | | | |
|---|---|---|---|
| A/an | 41 | Opposites | 31 |
| Abbreviations | 43 | Past | 20 |
| Adjectives | 9, 25, 26, 41 | Phrases | 19 |
| Adjectives, comparative | 38, 41 | Picture comprehension | 12 |
| Adverbs | 16, 17, 19 | Place words | 24 |
| Alphabetical order | 6, 13 | Plurals | 40-1, 47 |
| Am/is | 15 | Poems | 27 |
| Apostrophes, belonging | 34-35, 37 | Possessive apostrophes | 34-5, 37 |
| | | Possessive pronouns | 39, 41, 47 |
| Being verb | 15 | Prepositions | 24 |
| | | Present | 21 |
| Capital letters | 5 | Pronouns | 32-3, 37 |
| Collective nouns | 3, 13 | Proper nouns | 3, 9 |
| Commas | 5 | Punctuation revision | 4 |
| Common nouns | 3, 9, 25 | | |
| Comprehension | 44-5 | Question marks | 5, 31 |
| Conjunctions | 8, 9, 13 | | |
| | | Rhyming | 47 |
| Dictionary work | 7 | | |
| | | Saying words | 28 |
| Envelopes, addressing | 23 | Sentences | 4-5, 19 |
| | | Saying without words | 30 |
| Full stops | 5 | Sound-alike words | 46-7 |
| Future | 20-1, 25 | Spelling | 37 |
| | | Story writing | 2, 11, 29, 33 |
| Got | 10, 13 | | |
| | | Verbs | 9, 14-15, 19 |
| Instructions | 18, 36 | | 28  31 |
| | | Was/were | 15, 19 |
| Joining words | 8, 9, 13 | Wasted words | 42 |
| Letter writing | 22-3 | | |
| Nice | 10, 13 | | |
| Nouns | 3, 9, 13 | | |

Collins Educational

© Peter and Joan Moss

First published 1988. ISBN 0 00313322-2

All rights reserved. No part of this publication may be reproduced, stored in a retrieval system, or transmitted in any form or by any means, electronic, mechanical, photocopying, recording or otherwise, without the prior permission of the publisher.

**Acknowledgements**
Designed by David Armitage;
artwork by Bob Geary;
cover artwork by Toni Goffe.

The authors and publisher wish to thank the following for permission to reproduce copyright material:
Extract from **The Sea Egg** by L.M. Boston reprinted by permission of Faber and Faber Ltd p44; "Fat Cat" by Mary Rayner from **Allsorts 6** (Methuen Children's Books) p27.